Old

Seque

First Edition, 1947

Second Edition 1950 (*completely revised*)

OLD TIME AND SEQUENCE DANCES

Descriptions standardised by the
OFFICIAL BOARD OF
BALLROOM DANCING

ACKNOWLEDGMENTS

Various organisations represented on the Official Board of Ballroom Dancing appointed delegates to sit on the Old Time Committee. These delegates, all of whom put in countless hours in the selection and standardisation of the dances which this book contains, were as follows :—

ALLIED DANCING ASSOCIATION : Mr. J. Mercer, Miss L. Parry; ASSOCIATION OF BALLROOMS LTD. : Mr. M. Munro; BRITISH ASSOCIATION OF TEACHERS OF DANCING : Mr. A. Worrall, Miss D. Bullars; EMPIRE SOCIETY OF TEACHERS OF DANCING : Mr. A. Wantling, Mr. J. Evans; IMPERIAL SOCIETY OF TEACHERS OF DANCING : Miss C. Ruault, Miss S. Clarke; INTERNATIONAL DANCING MASTERS' ASSOCIATION : Mr. W. Collinson, Mme. P. Enderby; MIDLAND ASSOCIATION OF TEACHERS OF DANCING : Mr. G. Southcott, Mr. T. Smith; NATIONAL ASSOCIATION OF TEACHERS OF DANCING : Mr. A. Cowan (Chairman of the Committee), Mr. E. Macdonald; NORTH BRITISH BALLROOMS ASSOCIATION : Mr. E. Stewart; SCOTTISH DANCE TEACHERS' ALLIANCE : Mrs. N. Warren; UNITED KINGDOM ALLIANCE OF TEACHERS OF DANCING : Mr. H. BOYLE (Deputy Chairman of the Committee), Mrs. M. Fairley.

Special mention must be accorded to Miss Cecil Ruault and Mr. Edward MacDonald, who prepared the first draft to be used by the committee as a basis for the completion of the book.

Independent Members appointed to the Committee were Mr. William B. Arkley, Mr. Frank Bullars and Mr. Sydney Thompson.

Mrs. R. M. Ashdown, on behalf of the British Association of Teachers of Dancing, also attended several meetings.

Mrs. Dorothy Craig acted as secretary to the Committee.

CONTENTS

INTRODUCTION

This book has been compiled by the Old Time Committee of the Official Board of Ballroom Dancing. It is intended especially for the use of teachers and skilled dancers. The nine dances permissible in Old Time Championships are, it is true, covered in some detail, but not in sufficient detail to be fully understood by a novice. The remaining dances are described as briefly as possible for the fully fledged dancer. The Committee confidently believes that complete clarity in the descriptions has been achieved for all those who possess the pre-requisite knowledge and experience.

The gentleman's steps only have been described in all those cases where the lady's steps follow the " normal opposite " procedure; and in other cases where her steps are exactly similar to those of the man.

Very few abbreviations appear, and very few technical terms. All such terms as are defined in the *Dictionary compiled by this Board are shown in italics.

It may be thought by many, in view of the fact that this book is intended for experienced dancers, that descriptions of Holds are not necessary. The committee felt it advisable, however, to include brief descriptions of them for the purposes of completeness and reference. These Holds are described on pages 7 and 8.

In all dances in which Hold number 2 is used, provided the sequence terminates with a Waltz Turn, the standard ending as described for the Veleta should be adopted.

ALBERT COWAN,
Chairman, Old Time Committee,
Official Board of Ballroom Dancing.

* OLD TIME AND SEQUENCE DANCING : A Short Dictionary of Technical Terms.

THE HOLDS

In order to avoid unnecessary repetition all the Holds used in Old Time Dancing are described here. At the beginning of the description of each dance the number of the appropriate Hold is given.

Number 1

Partners face each other, slightly apart. The gentleman extends his left arm at about shoulder level, with the elbow curved and the palm of his hand inward and upward. His partner rests her right hand in his left. The gentleman's right hand passes round his partner so that his right hand rests gently but firmly on her back, just below her left shoulder-blade. This position of the gentleman's right hand may be adjusted slightly in accordance with the height and build both of himself and his partner. The lady's left hand rests on her partner's right upper arm.

Number 2

Partners stand side by side and face almost along Line of Dance, turning very slightly inwards towards each other. The gentleman places his left foot and the lady her right in third position front. The lady's left hand is held in her partner's right hand, his palm upward, slightly higher than his shoulder. The elbows must be slightly curved. The gentleman places his left hand lightly on his hip and the lady holds her gown with the right hand.

Number 3

Both face Line of Dance, lady's left hand in gentleman's left, her right hand in his right, slightly above shoulder level. The gentleman's right shoulder is kept behind his partner's left shoulder.

Number 4

This Hold follows the general lines of that laid down for number 1 except that the partners stand in contact with each other. The gentleman raises his left forearm so that it is pointing almost, but not quite, straight upward.

Number 5

Face each other, sideways to L.O.D., arms extended to sides, elbows slightly curved at approximately shoulder level. Gentleman's hands palm upwards and inwards. Lady's right hand rests in gentleman's left hand, lady's left hand in gentleman's right hand.

Number 6

Both face L.O.D., side by side. Gentleman takes lady's right hand in his right hand and her left hand in his left hand, joining hands across the body, elbows slightly curved and left hands above right hands.

Number 7

Both face L.O.D., side by side. Gentleman's right arm round lady's waist, lady's right wrist in gentleman's right hand. Lady's left hand rests in gentleman's left hand, approximately shoulder high.

CHAMPIONSHIP   DANCES

WALTZ

Time : 3/4.   Tempo : 48 bars a minute.

Starting position : Gentleman starts with his back to the centre with L.F. in 3rd position rear, and lady starts facing centre with R.F. in 3rd position front.

Hold : No. 1 as described on page 7.

	Count	
Natural Turn		
Glide L.F. diagonally to wall on ball of foot, beginning to turn to the right.	1	
Toe of R.F. to heel of L.F., in 5th position rear, still turning.	2	Lady's 2nd half
Pivoting on balls of both feet to face diagonally to centre, finish with weight on L.F. with R.F. in 5th position front.	3	
R.F. forward along L.O.D., with ball-heel lead, still turning.	1	
L.F. to side slightly back from L.O.D., still turning.	2	Lady's 1st half
Close R.F. to L.F. in 5th position front, completing the turn.	3	
Reverse Turn		
Start facing L.O.D.		
L.F. forward with ball-heel lead, along L.O.D. beginning to turn to left.	1	
R.F. to side, slightly back from L.O.D. still turning.	2	Lady's 2nd half
Close L.F. to R.F. in 5th position front, still turning, to back diagonally to wall.	3	

9

	Count	
R.F. back and slightly sideways, still turning.	1	
Toe of L.F. to heel of R.F. in 5th position rear, still turning.	2	Lady's 1st half
Pivot on balls of both feet, finishing with weight on R.F. with L.F. in 5th position front, to complete the turn.	3	

Both in the Natural and Reverse Turns the body turns throughout.

Pas de Valse

This figure may be started with either foot, and danced forward or backward.

The following illustration is begun with the L.F. :—

Forward

	Count
L.F. forward with ball-heel lead.	1
R.F. forward on ball of foot with slight right shoulder lead.	2
Close L.F. to R.F. on ball of foot in 3rd position rear, lowering left heel at end of step.	3

Backward

L.F. back on ball of foot.	1
R.F. back on ball of foot with slight right shoulder lead.	2
Close L.F. to R.F. in 3rd position front, lowering left heel at end of step	3

Amalgamation : First three steps Natural Turn, Fwd. Pas de Valse, Reverse Turn, Fwd. Pas de Valse, last three steps Natural Turn.

VELETA

Arranged by Arthur Morris.

Music published by Francis, Day & Hunter, Ltd.

Time : 3/4.   Tempo : 46 bars a minute.

Hold : No. 2 as described on page 7.

	Count	Bars
L.F. forward, with ball-heel lead, beginning to carry the raised arm forward.	1	
R.F. forward, on ball of foot, turning outward from each other.	2	
Close L.F. to R.F. on ball of foot, in third position rear, lowering left heel at end of step.	3	1
R.F. forward, with ball-heel lead, beginning to carry the raised arm to the rear.	1	
L.F. forward, on ball of foot, turning inward to face wall.	2	
Close R.F. to L.F. in third position front, lowering heel at end of step and turning to face against L.O.D. Gentleman is now backing diagonally to centre and lady backing diagonally to wall.	3	2
Reverse the position of the arms.		
L.F. sideways along L.O.D., on ball of foot, lowering left heel as weight is transferred over left leg and begin to draw R.F. with pressure on ball of foot towards L.F.	1-2	
Close R.F. to L.F. in third position front, lowering right heel at end of step.	3	3
Repeat bar 3 without transferring weight on the last step.		4
Repeat Bars 1-4 against L.O.D. beginning with R.F.		5-8

	Count	Bars

2 bars Natural Waltz Turn, with normal Waltz hold. — **9 and 10**

Opening out to face against L.O.D., repeat bars 3 and 4, but transfer weight to R.F. at end of last step. — **11 and 12**

Adopt Waltz hold. Gentleman dances 3 bars Natural Waltz and 1 bar *Pas de Valse*, finishing with R.F. in third position rear. Lady dances 4 bars Natural Waltz, finishing with R.F. in third position front. — **13-16**

Both lady and gentleman finish in original positions.

MILITARY TWO STEP

Arranged by James Finnigan.

Music published by Francis, Day & Hunter.

Time : 6/8.   Tempo : 56 bars a minute.

Hold : No. 2 as described on page 7, but both facing L.O.D.

	Count	Bars
Point L.F. forward, heel raised.	1, 2	1

Point L.F. to 5th position rear, with heel raised, turning towards partner. Acknowledge each other, keeping hands joined. — 1, 2 — 2

Turning to face L.O.D. walk three steps forward with heel lead; L.F., R.F., L.F. — 1, 2, 1

Pivot inward with feet still apart to face against L.O.D. Reverse joined hands. Lady now holds her skirt with her left hand and gentleman has right hand down to his side. — 2 — 3 and 4

Point R.F. forward, heel raised. — 1, 2 — 5

Turn and face each other, gentleman closing R.F. to L.F. (*parallel position*). Lady swings her L.F. in a

12

	Count	Bars
semi-circle to the rear and makes a full curtsey. At the same time gentleman gives a military salute with his right hand.	1, 2	6
Keeping right hand at side, turn to face against L.O.D. Walk three steps forward with heel lead : R.F., L.F., R.F.	1, 2, 1	
Turn inward to face partner. Close L.F. to R.F. in parallel position without transferring weight.	2	7 and 8
Adopting Waltz hold gentleman completes 7 bars Natural Waltz turn and 1 bar *Pas de Valse,* finishing with R.F. in 3rd position rear. Lady completes 8 bars Natural Waltz Turn, finishing with R.F. in 3rd position front. Both finish facing L.O.D. in original position.		9-16

BOSTON TWO STEP

Arranged by Tom Walton.

Music published by Francis, Day & Hunter.

Time : 6/8.   Tempo : 56 bars a minute.

Hold : No. 2 as described on page 7, but both facing L.O.D.

	Count	Bars
Pas de Basque outward starting with L.F. (i.e., L.F. to side with a springing action, the foot making a circular motion. Bring R.F. to L.F. in 5th position front, with heel raised. Replace weight on to L.F. with a sharp cutting action, raising R.F. in front with the toe pointing downward).	1 and 2	1
Pas de Basque inward starting with R.F.	1 and 2	2
Walk three steps forward with heel lead : L.F., R.F., L.F.	1, 2, 1	

13

	Count	Bars
Pivot inward with feet still apart to face against L.O.D. at the same time reversing position of hands.	2	3 and 4
Pas de Basque outward starting with R.F.	1 and 2	5
Pas de Basque inward starting with L.F.	1 and 2	6
Walk three steps with heel lead, against L.O.D. : R.F., L.F., R.F.	1, 2, 1	
Turn inward to face partner, closing L.F. to R.F. without transferring weight, in *parallel position,* and with both hands joined. Gentleman is now facing wall and lady facing centre.	2	7 and 8
Pas de Basque starting with L.F.	1 and 2	9
Pas de Basque starting with R.F.	1 and 2	10
L.F. to side	1	
Close R.F. to L.F. in parallel position.	2	11
Repeat last two steps.	1 and 2	12
Adopting Waltz hold, complete 4 bars Natural Waltz Turn. Lady completes turn and finishes with R.F. in 3rd position front. Gentleman opens out on last bar with a *Pas de Valse,* finishing with R.F. in 3rd position rear.		
Both finish facing L.O.D., in original position, ready to repeat.		13-16

14

ROYAL EMPRESS TANGO

Arranged by Adele Roscoe and H. Clifton.

Music published by B. Feldman & Co. Ltd.

Time : 2/4.   Tempo : 32 bars a minute.

Hold : No. 4 as described on page 8.

	Count	Bars
Walk and Chasse.		
Two steps forward, L.F., R.F., with over relaxation of right knee on last step.	S.S	1
Two steps back, L.F., R.F., with slight relaxation of right knee on last step.	S.S	2
L.F. forward diagonally to centre. Close R.F. to L.F., L.F. forward diagonally to centre, turning to right at end of step to face diagonally to wall.	Q.Q.S	3
Repeat 3rd bar diagonally to wall turning on the last step to face square to centre in *Promenade Position.*	Q.Q.S	4
Promenade and Chasse.		
Two steps forward, L.F., R.F., towards centre in *Promenade Position.*	S.S	5
Chassé, L.F., R.F., L.F., still in *Promenade Position,* turning on end of last step to face wall. At the same time curve left arm inward.	Q.Q.S	6
Repeat 5th and 6th bars towards wall in *Counter Promenade Position,* starting with R.F., turning at end of last step to face L.O.D. in *Promenade Position,* bringing arms back to normal.	S.S.Q.Q.S	7 and 8

15

	Count	Bars

Promenade and Pivot.

Two steps in *Promenade Position* along L.O.D.. L.F., R.F., turning to right on last step. *Pivot* to right in two steps, L.F., R.F., finishing in *Promenade Position,* facing L.O.D. (On 3rd step gentleman steps across L.O.D. with L.F. Lady steps forward with R.F. between gentleman's feet.)

| S.S.S.S. | 9 and 10 |

Promenade Swivel and Point.

Two steps in *Promenade Position* : L.F., R.F.

| S.S | 11 |

Point L.F. along L.O.D. with heel raised and knee relaxed and swivel inward to face against L.O.D. with feet still apart (weight has now been transferred to L.F. and R.F. is pointing against L.O.D.). At the same time curve left arm inward.

| S.S | 12 |

Repeat 11th and 12th bars, starting with R.F. and finish facing L.O.D., bringing arms back to normal.

| S.S.S.S | 13 and 14 |

Rotary Chassé.

Two *Chassés* : L.F., R.F., L.F. (side, close, back) R.F., L.F., R.F. (side, close, forward), turning to right and finishing in starting position, facing L.O.D.

| Q.Q.S.Q.Q.S | 15 and 16 |

All forward and promenade walks and forward Chassés are taken with a heel lead.

Where one foot closes to the other the feet are in parallel position : toe to toe, heel to heel.

LATCHFORD SCHOTTISCHE

Arranged by Madame M. Oldbury.

Music published by Francis, Day & Hunter Ltd.

Time : 4/4.   Tempo : 26 bars a minute.

Hold : No. 2 as described on page 7.

	Count	Bars
Glide L.F. forward on ball of foot, lowering heel at end of step.	1	
Close R.F. to 3rd position rear.	2	
Glide L.F. forward on ball of foot, lowering heel at end of step.	3	
Point R.F. to 4th position front.	4	1
Glide R.F. back to 4th position rear, on ball of foot, lowering heel at end of step.	1	
Close L.F. to 3rd position front, lowering heel at end of step.	2	
Glide R.F. back to 4th position rear, on ball of foot, lowering heel at end of step.	3	
Close L.F. to 3rd position front, without changing weight or lowering left heel.	4	2
Pas de Basque outward, starting with L.F. (as in Boston Two Step).	1 and 2	
Pas de Basque inward starting with R.F.	3 and 4	3
(At end of 3rd bar, release hands, but keep them at the same angle and height throughout 4th bar.)		
Solo Waltz outward (gentleman Reverse Turn) starting with L.F.	1 and 2	
Lady Natural Turn starting with R.F.	3 and 4	4

	Count	Bars

Rejoining hands, repeat 1st and 2nd bars. — 5 and 6

Repeat 4th bar. — 7

Gentleman bows, lady curtsies, holding skirt in right hand, with left arm raised, as follows :—

Gentleman :

Turning to face partner L.F. to side into 2nd position along L.O.D. — 1

Close R.F. to 3rd position front, without transferring weight, making slight bow and bringing right hand across the body and left hand slightly away from body. — 2

R.F. diagonally forward. — 3

Close L.F. to 3rd position rear, without transferring weight. — 4 — 8

Lady :

Turning to face partner, R.F. to side into 2nd position along L.O.D. — 1

Curtsey, taking L.F. with slight *Rond de Jambe* to 4th position rear, keeping weight on R.F. — 2

L.F. diagonally forward. — 3

Close R.F. to 3rd position front, without transferring weight. — 4 — 8

Adopt Waltz hold.

Gentleman dances $3\frac{1}{2}$ bars Natural Waltz completing 4th bar with *Pas de Valse*, finishing with R.F. in 3rd position rear. Lady dances 4 bars Natural Waltz, finishing with R.F. in 3rd position front. — 9-12

Both lady and gentleman finish in original position.

18

LOLA TANGO

Arranged by Arthur Wantling.

Music published by Francis, Day & Hunter Ltd.

Time : 2/4.   Tempo : 32 bars a minute.

Hold : No. 4 as described on page 8.

	Count	Bars
Four steps forward. L.F., R.F., L.F., R.F. Close L.F. to R.F.	S.S.S.Q.Q	1 and 2
Four steps forward : R.F., L.F., R.F., L.F. Close R.F. to L.F. On the last step, open into *Promenade Position,* facing diagonally to centre.	S.S.S.Q.Q	3 and 4
Five steps diagonally to centre, L.F., R.F., L.F., R.F., L.F., still in *Promenade Position.* Close R.F. to L.F., without transferring weight, *pivoting* to face diagonally to wall against L.O.D.	S.S.Q.Q.Q.Q	5 and 6
Repeat 5th and 6th bars diagonally to wall against L.O.D. in *Counter Promenade Position,* finishing square to partner and facing diagonally to wall.	S.S.Q.Q.Q.Q	7 and 8
L.F. forward turning to left. Side R.F. facing diagonally to centre. Close L.F. to R.F.	S.Q.Q	9
R.F. back. Transfer weight forward on to L.F.	S.S	10
Repeat 9th and 10th bars, starting with R.F. and turning to face diagonally to wall.	S.Q.Q.S.S	11 and 12
Two steps back diagonally to centre against L.O.D. : L.F., R.F. On last step brush L.F. to R.F. opening into *Promenade Position,* facing L.O.D.	S.S	13

19

	Count	Bars

Two steps in *Promenade Position* along L.O.D. : L.F., R.F., turning to right on last step. *Pivot* to right in two steps, L.F., R.F., finishing square to partner, facing L.O.D. (On 3rd step gentleman steps across L.O.D. with L.F. Lady steps forward between gentleman's feet with R.F.   S.S.S.S   14 and 15

Two steps forward, L.F., R.F.   Q.Q

L.F. to side, a short step, and close R.F. to L.F.   Q.Q   16

All forward and Promenade Walks and forward Chassés are taken with a heel lead. Where one foot closes to the other the feet are in parallel position, toe to toe, heel to heel.

MOONLIGHT SAUNTER

Arranged by C. J. Daniels.

Music published by Hermann Darewski.

Time : 4/4. Tempo : 28 bars a minute.

Hold : No. 1 as described on page 7.

	Count	Bars

Four steps forward : L.F., R.F., L.F., R.F. (heel lead). Swivel one eighth turn to right at the end of the 4th step to face diagonally to wall.   S.S.S.S   1 and 2

L.F. forward outside partner on her left side. Place R.F. to side on ball of foot without weight, swivel one eighth turn to right to face L.O.D. (now square to partner).   S.S   4

20

R.F. forward outside partner on her right side.   Place L.F. to side on ball of foot without weight, swivel one eighth turn to right to face L.O.D. (now square to partner).   S.S   4

Repeat bars 1-4.   5-8

Two steps forward: L.F., R.F., L.F. forward, with slight relaxation, leaving R.F. in open position. Transfer weight over R.F.   S.S.S.S   9 and 10

Brush L.F. to R.F. and side L.F. Close R.F. to L.F.   L.F. back.   Q.Q.S   11

Brush R.F. to L.F. and side R.F. Close L.F. to R.F.   R.F. forward.   Q.Q.S   12

Repeat bars 9-12, turning on last step into *Promenade Position* to face L.O.D.   13-16

In the following 4 bars (Nos. 17-20) the lady's steps differ from those of her partner; they are described at the end of bar No. 20.

Two steps forward in *Promenade Position*, L.F., R.F., starting to turn to right at end of 2nd step.   S.S   17

L.F. to side across L.O.D. still turning.   Point R.F. along L.O.D. in *Counter Promenade Position*.   S.S   18

Two steps forward in *Counter Promenade Position*, R.F., L.F.   S.S   19
R.F. forward between partner's feet, turning to right.   S

Point L.F. along L.O.D. in *Promenade Position*.   S   20

Lady's steps for bars numbered 17-20.

Two steps in *Promenade Position*, R.F., L.F.   R.F. between partner's

21

	Count	Bars
feet, turning to right. Point L.F. along L.O.D. in *Counter Promenade Position*.	S.S.S.S	17 and 18
Two steps in *Counter Promenade Position*, L.F., R.F., turning to right on 2nd step. L.F. to side across L.O.D., still turning. Point R.F. along L.O.D. in *Promenade Position*.	S.S.S.S	19 and 20
Repeat bars 17-20.		21-24
Two steps forward, L.F., R.F., in *Promenade Position* along L.O.D.	S.S	25
Balancé forward over L.F. Close R.F. to 3rd position rear without transferring weight.	S	
Step back with R.F., closing and pointing L.F. to 5th position front.	S	26
Two steps forward, L.F., R.F., turning to right on 2nd step.	S.S	27
L.F. across L.O.D. (now square to partner) and *pivot* to right. R.F. forward along L.O.D. finishing in *Promenade Position*.	S.S	28
Repeat bars 25-28, finishing square to partner and facing L.O.D. at end of last bar.		29-32

All forward and Promenade Walks and forward Chassés are taken with a heel lead. Where one foot closes to the other the feet are in parallel position, toe to toe, heel to heel, unless otherwise stated.

DESTINY WALTZ

Arranged by the Old Time Committee of the " Official Board."

Music published by Swann & Co.

Time : 3/4.   Tempo : 52 bars a minute.

Hold : No. 1 as described on page 7.

	Count	Bars
Four steps forward : L.F., R.F., L.F., R.F. Each step is taken with a ball-heel lead, but with smooth gliding movements and slight lilt.		1-4
First three steps of Reverse Waltz Turn, starting with L.F. Finish backing L.O.D.		5
Balance back on R.F., closing L.F. to 3rd position front without transferring weight.		6
Balance forward on L.F., closing R.F. to 3rd position rear without transferring weight.		7
Balance back on R.F., closing L.F. to 3rd position front without transferring weight.		8
Repeat bars 1-8 against L.O.D., turning into *Promenade Position* at end of 16th bar. Gentleman's L.F. and lady's R.F. now in 3rd position front.		9-16
Two steps forward in *Promenade Position* along L.O.D. : L.F., R.F.		17 and 18
L.F. forward along L.O.D., still in *Promenade Position.*	1, 2	
R.F. forward along L.O.D., still in *Promenade Position.*	3	

23

	Count	Bars

L.F. forward along L.O.D. still in *Promenade Position,* turning at end of step to face against L.O.D. — Count 1

Close R.F. to 3rd position front without transferring weight, lowering heel of L.F. — Count 2, 3 — Bars 19 and 20

' Ball of foot lead is used throughout last two bars.

Repeat bars 17-20 against L.O.D. starting with R.F. and finishing to face wall. — Bars 21-24

Waltz Natural Turn (approximately 3½ turns) and finish with a *Pas de Valse* along L.O.D. — Bars 25-32

ROUND DANCES

BARN DANCE

Time : 4/4.   Tempo : 32 bars a minute.

Hold : No. 2 as described on page 7.

	Count	Bars
Glide L.F. forward.	1	
Close R.F. to 3rd position rear.	2	
Glide L.F. forward.	3	
Hop lightly on L.F., bringing R.F. to 4th position front (aerial).	4	1
Repeat 1st bar starting with R.F., turning towards partner on 3rd and 4th beats.		2
Adopt Waltz hold.		
Waltz Natural Turn 1½ bars, and finish in starting position with a *Pas de Valse*		3 and 4
Lady dances 2 bars Natural Waltz, finishing with R.F. in 3rd position front.		

25

CARINA WALTZ

Arranged by Tom Hayton.

Music published by Francis, Day & Hunter.

Time : 3/4.   Tempo : 48 bars a minute.

Hold : No. 2 as described on page 7.

	Bars
Point L.F. first forward and then back.	1 and 2
L.F. forward, close R.F. to L.F. L.F. forward and turn to face against L.O.D.	3 and 4
Repeat bars 1-4 starting with R.F. Finish with L.F. in 3rd position front and facing to wall.	5-8
Now holding both hands.	
Two steps forward towards wall : L.F., R.F. Two steps forward in *Promenade Position* : L.F., R.F.	9-12
Waltz Natural Turns.	13-16

CHRYSANTHEMUM WALTZ

Arranged by James Telford and A. Bell.

Time : 3/4.   Tempo : 46/48 bars a minute.

Hold : No. 1 as described on page 7.

	Bars
Two steps forward in *Promenade Position* : L.F., R.F.	1 and 2
With a circling movement bring L.F. to 4th position front (aerial), with knee bent and toe pointing to the floor.	3
Step on to L.F. pivoting inward to face opposite direction with R.F. pointing against L.O.D.	4
In Counter *Promenade Position* repeat bars 1-4 against L.O.D., starting with R.F. finishing to face partner. (Gentleman now facing wall.)	5-8

	Bars
L.F. to side along L.O.D. and close R.F. to L.F.	9
Repeat 9th bar, closing R.F. to L.F .without transferring weight.	10
Repeat 9th and 10th bars against L.O.D. starting with R.F.	11 and 12
Release Waltz hold and join both hands, arms extended. L.F. to side.	13
Cross R.F. behind L.F., without transferring weight, with slight relaxation of both knees. (Lady also crosses behind.)	14
R.F. to side against L.O.D.	15
Cross L.F. behind R.F., without transferring weight, with slight relaxation of both knees. Release lady's right hand.	16
Pas de Valse forward as in Veleta : L.F., R.F., L.F.	17
Balancé forward on R.F.	18
Repeat 17th and 18th bars backward, starting with L.F.	19 and 20
Two steps forward : L.F., R.F.	21 and 22
Solo Waltz outward, starting with L.F.	23 and 24
(Gentleman : one complete Reverse Turn. Lady : one complete Natural Turn.) Both now facing L.O.D., gentleman holding lady's left hand in his right hand.	
Point L.F. forward.	25
Point L.F. to side.	26
Point L.F. back.	27
Close L.F. to R.F., without transferring weight, turning to face partner.	28
Adopt Waltz hold.	
Complete two Waltz Natural Turns.	29-32

27

DEVONIA

Arranged by W. Lugg.

Music published by the Orpheus Publishing Co.

Time : 3/4.   Tempo : 48 bars.

Hold : No. 2 as described on page 7.

	Bars
L.F. forward. R.F. to 4th position front (aerial). Raise heel of L.F., then lower.	1
Point R.F. to 4th position front.	2
Repeat 1st and 2nd bars, starting with R.F.	3 and 4
Solo Waltz outward, starting with L.F.	5 and 6
Repeat 1st and 2nd bars.	7 and 8
Repeat bars 1-8, starting with R.F., turning inward on Solo Waltz.	9-16
Pas de basque, starting with L.F. moving forward, R.F. back.	17
Close L.F. to R.F. without transferring weight.	18
Repeat 17th and 18th bars.	19 and 20
Gentleman now releases lady's left hand from his right and takes her right hand in his left.	
L.F. to side along L.O.D. *pivoting* to right on L.F. and keeping R.F. off the floor.	21
Partners are now back to back.	
R.F. to side along L.O.D., close L.F. to R.F.	22
R.F. to side along L.O.D. *pivoting* to left to face partner, gentleman still holding lady's right hand in his left hand.	23
L.F. to side and close R.F. to L.F.	24
Adopt Waltz hold.	
Half Waltz Turn, changing places with partner.	25
R.F. to side, close L.F. to R.F.	26
Half Waltz Turn back to place.	27
L.F. to side, close R.F. to L.F.	28
Natural Waltz Turn.	29-32

DINKY ONE STEP

Time : 2/4.   Tempo : 56 bars a minute.

Hold : No. 4 as described on page 8.

	Count	Bars
Point L.F. forward.	1, 2	1
Point L.F. back.	1, 2	2
Four steps forward : L.F., R.F., L.F., R.F.	1, 2, 1, 2	3 and 4
Repeat bars 1-4.		5-8
Point L.F. to side.	1	
Close L.F. to R.F.	2	9
Point R.F. to side.	1	
Close R.F. to L.F.	2	10
L.F. to side (step).	1	
Close R.F. to L.F. without transferring weight.	2	11
R.F. to side (step).	1	
Close L.F. to R.F. without transferring weight.	2	12
Four steps forward : L.F., R.F., L.F., R.F.	1, 2, 1, 2	
Complete a full turn to the right : L.F., R.F., L.F., R.F.	1, 2, 1, 2	13-16

DONELLA TANGO

Time : 2/4.   Tempo : 32 bars a minute.

Hold : No. 4 as described on page 8.

	Count	Bars
L.F. forward.	S	
Close R.F. to L.F. without transferring weight.	S	1
R.F. forward.	S	
Close L.F. to R.F. without transferring weight.	S	2

	Count	Bars
Repeat 1st and 2nd bars.		3 and 4
L.F. forward diagonally to centre, preparing to step outside partner.	S	
R.F. forward outside partner on her right side.	S	5
L.F. back turning to right to face wall. Square to partner.	S	
R.F. to side, still turning.	Q	
Close L.F. to R.F. to face diagonally to wall against L.O.D.	Q	6
Repeat 5th and 6th bars diagonally to wall against L.O.D., starting with R.F. and stepping outside lady's left side. Finish in *Promenade Position* facing along L.O.D.	S.S.S.Q.Q	7 and 8
Two steps *Promenade Position*: L.F., R.F. turning square to partner on last step.	S.S	9
Two steps back to centre: L.F., R.F.	S.S	10
Two steps forward towards wall: L.F., R.F.	S.S	11
Pivot to right to face L.O.D.: L.F., R.F.	S.S	12
Four steps forward: L.F., R.F., L.F., R.F.	S.S.S.S	13 and 14
Cross L.F. over R.F. turning slightly to right.	S	
(Lady crosses R.F. behind L.F.) Point R.F. to side.	S	15
Cross R.F. over L.F. turning slightly to left. (Lady crosses behind).	S	15
Close L.F. to R.F., without transferring weight, to face L.O.D.	S	16

DORIS WALTZ

Arranged by J. Bickerstaffe.

Music published by W. Paxton & Co. Ltd.

Time : 3/4. Tempo : 48 bars a minute.

Hold : No. 3 as described on page 7.

	Bars
Balance diagonally forward on L.F. along L.O.D. and close R.F. to 3rd position rear without transferring weight.	1
Balance back on R.F. and close L.F. to 3rd position front without transferring weight.	2
Chassé forward : L.F., R.F., L.F. Turn on last step to face diagonally to wall against L.O.D.	3 and 4
Repeat bars 1-4 starting with R.F.	5-8
Finish facing each other, gentleman facing wall and lady facing centre, with right hands joined. (On last bar lady makes a pivot turn to her left under gentleman's right arm.)	
Retaining hold with right hands, balance backward away from each other, on L.F. Balance forward on R.F.	9 and 10
Repeat 9th and 10th bars. (Lady transfers weight to L.F. at end of last bar.)	11 and 12
Adopt Waltz hold.	
Waltz Natural Turn, adopting starting position on last bar.	13-16

ESPERANO BARN DANCE

Arranged by T. Almond.

Music published by Francis, Day & Hunter, Ltd.

Time : 4/4. Tempo : 28 bars a minute.

Hold : No. 2 as described on page 7.

	Count	Bars
Glide L.F. forward (ball of foot).	1	
R.F. to 3rd position rear.	2	
Glide L.F. forward (ball of foot).	3	

	Count	Bars
Turn inward and point R.F. towards partner.	4	1
Natural Waltz Turn, starting with R.F. and turning lady under right arm, changing hands at end of second half of turn. (Lady makes Reverse Turn starting with L.F.)	1 and 2 3 and 4	2
Partners are now in opposite places.		
Repeat 1st and 2nd bars, starting with R.F.		3 and 4
Glide L.F. forward.	1	
Close R.F. to L.F. in 3rd position rear.	2	
Glide L.F. forward.	3	
Hop lightly on L.F. bringing R.F. forward to 4th position front (aerial).	4	5
Step on to R.F., L.F. to side (small step), close R.F. to 5th position front.	1 and 2	
Glide L.F. to side and close R.F. to L.F. in 5th position.	3 and 4	6
Adopt Waltz hold.		
Waltz Natural Turn.		7 and 8

EVA THREE STEP

Arranged by Sydney Walter Painter, Senior.

Time : 4/4.   Tempo : 28 bars a minute.

Hold : No. 2 as described on page 7.

	Count	Bars
Three steps forward : L.F., R.F., L.F.	1, 2, 3	
Pause.	4	1
Three steps sideways to right. R.F., L.F., R.F. Change hold on 2nd step, gentleman taking lady's left hand in his left, than passing her under his left arm on 3rd step.	1, 2, 3	

	Count	Bars
Pause.	4	2
Release hands.		
Three steps diagonally forward to left : L.F., R.F., L.F.	1, 2, 3	
(Lady : three steps diagonally backward to right : R.F., L.F., R.F.)		
Pause.	4	3
Three steps back to original position : R.F., L.F., R.F.	1, 2, 3	
(Lady. three steps forward to original position : L.F., R.F., L.F.)		
Pause.	4	4
Solo Waltz outward (i.e., gentleman reverse, lady natural). Finish facing partner and join both hands.	1 and 2 3 and 4	5
L.F. to side along L.O.D.	1	
Swing R.F. across L.F.	2	6
R.F. to side against L.O.D.	3	
Swing L.F. across R.F.	4	
Adopt Waltz hold.		
Waltz Natural Turn.		7 and 8

FLORENTINE WALTZ

Time : 3/4.   Tempo : 48 bars a minute.

Hold : No. 1 as described on page 7.

	Bars
L.F. forward along L.O.D. in *Promenade Position*. Cross R.F. over L.F. L.F. forward, *Pivoting* to face against L.O.D. Point R.F. against L.O.D.	1-4
Repeat bars 1-4 against L.O.D. starting with R.F. and finishing to face L.O.D.	5-8
Release hold.	
Solo Waltz outward starting with L.F. and finish facing wall. Join both hands.	9 and 10
L.F. a short step to side along L.O.D. Swing R.F. over L.F. without transferring weight.	11

33

R.F. a short step to side against L.O.D. Swing
L.F. over R.F. without transferring weight.　　　　12

Repeat bars 9-12.　　　　13-16

Join right hands.

Three steps forward towards wall : L.F., R.F.,
L.F. (Lady towards Centre : R.F., L.F., R.F.)
On 3rd step turn to face each other, gentleman
facing centre and turning the lady under his arm.
Bow and curtsey.　　　　17-20

Repeat bars 17-20 back to original places, gentleman starting with L.F. and lady with R.F.　　　　21-24

Join both hands.

R.F. over L.F., L.F. over R.F., R.F. over L.F.,
point L.F. along L.O.D.　　　　25-28

Adopt Waltz hold.

Natural Waltz Turn.　　　　29-32

FYLDE WALTZ

Arranged by T. Almond.

Time : 3/4.　Tempo : 48 bars a minute.

Hold : No. 2 as described on page 7.

	Count	Bars
Pas de Valse forward, starting with L.F.	1, 2, 3	1
Balance forward on R.F. raising right arm and close L.F. to 3rd position rear.	1, 2, 3	2
L.F. back. R.F. to 3rd position front, lowering arm.	1, 2, 3	3
L.F. back, starting to turn to right. Right toe behind left heel, *Pivot* on balls of both feet to face against L.O.D. R.F. now in 5th position front (half Waltz Turn). Change hands on 3rd beat.	1, 2, 3	4
Repeat bars 1-4 against L.O.D. starting with R.F.		5-8

Now facing L.O.D. half Reverse
Turn outward, finishing back to back.

34

	Count	Bars
(Gentleman's left hand and lady's right hand joined.)	1, 2, 3	9
R.F. back along L.O.D. Close L.F. to 3rd position front.	1, 2, 3	10
R.F. back along L.O.D. starting to turn inward. Left toe behind right heel, *Pivot* on balls of both feet to face partner. L.F. now in 5th position front. (Half Waltz Turn.)	1, 2, 3	11
Join both hands. Side L.F. Close R.F. to 3rd position front.	1, 2, 3	12
Adopt Waltz hold. Waltz Natural Turn opening out on the last bar to starting position.		13-16

THE GAY GORDONS

Time : 6/8.   Tempo : 56 bars a minute.
Hold : No. 3 as described on page 7.

	Bars
Four steps forward along L.O.D.: L.F., R.F. L.F., R.F., *Pivoting* on 4th step to face against L.O.D.	1 and 2
Four steps back along L.O.D. : L.F., R.F., L.F., R.F.	3 and 4
Repeat bars 1-4 against L.O.D.	5-8
Gentleman releases lady's left hand, and places his left hand on his hip. Four steps along L.O.D. : L.F., R.F., L.F., R.F., turning lady under his right arm. (Lady makes two complete turns to the right, pivoting R.F., L.F., R.F., L.F., under gentleman's right arm.) Finish to face each other, both hands joined.	9 and 10
Side L.F. along L.O.D. and close R.F. to L.F.	11
Repeat 11th bar.	12
(Lady : R.F. to side, close L.F. to R.F., side R.F., close L.F. to R.F.)	
Adopt Waltz hold. Waltz Natural Turn, turning on last bar into starting position.	13-16

GLEN MONA

Arranged by George Chester.

Music published by Reid Bros. Ltd.

Time : 4/4.   Tempo : 28 bars a minute.

Hold : No. 5 as described on page 8.

	Count	Bars
Balance forward on L.F.	1, 2	
Balance back on R.F.	3, 4	1
L.F. forward.	1	
Point R.F. first forward and then back.	2, 3	
Pivot inward to face against L.O.D. with weight on L.F.	4	2
(R.F. now pointing against L.O.D. with right hands lowered and left hands raised.)		
R.F. forward against L.O.D.	1, 2	
Point L.F. forward.	3, 4	3
L.F. forward.	1	
Point R.F. forward.	2	
Point R.F. back with slight dip.	3	
R.F. towards L.F. without transferring weight, straightening knees.	4	4
R.F. forward.	1, 2	
L.F. forward, *Pivoting* inward at end of step to face L.O.D.	3, 4	5
Point R.F. forward.	1, 2	
R.F. forward.	3	
Point L.F. to side, turning to face partner.	4	6
Adopt Waltz hold.		
Waltz Natural Turn		7 and 8

HESITATION WALTZ

Time : 3/4.   Tempo : 48 bars a minute.

Hold : No. 1 as described on page 7.

	Bars
Two steps back towards centre : L.F., R.F.	1 and 2
Two steps forward towards wall : L.F., R.F.	3 and 4
Chassé sideways to left along L.O.D. (L.F. to side, close R.F. to L.F., L.F. to side).	5 and 6
Turning into *Promenade Position*, R.F. forward over L.F. and L.F. forward, turning at end of step to face partner.	7 and 8
Repeat bars 1-8, starting with R.F.	9-16
Natural Waltz Turn.	17 and 18
Turning into *Promenade Position*, L.F. forward along L.O.D. and R.F. forward over L.F.	19 and 20
Repeat 17th and 18th bars.	21 and 22
Repeat 19th and 20th bars.	23 and 24
Facing wall, *Chassé* back towards centre. (L.F. back, close R.F. to L.F., L.F. back.)	25 and 26
Repeat 25th and 26th bars forward towards wall, starting with R.F.	27 and 28
Natural Waltz Turns.	29-32

HIGHLAND SCHOTTISCHE

Time : 4/4.   Tempo : 32 bars a minute.

Starting position : Gentleman backing centre.

Hold : No. 1 as described on page 7 in *Promenade Position*.

	Count	Bars
Hop on R.F., pointing L.F. in 2nd position.	1	
Hop on R.F. raising L.F. to 5th position (aerial) rear.	2	
Hop on R.F. pointing L.F. in 2nd position.	3	
Hop on R.F. raising L.F. to 5th position (aerial) front.	4	1
L.F. to side.	1	

	Count	Bars
Close R.F. to L.F. in 3rd position rear.	2	
L.F. to side.	3	
Hop on L.F. raising R.F. to 5th position (aerial) rear.	4	2
Repeat 1st and 2nd bars with opposite foot.		3 and 4

(In *Counter Promenade Position.*)

	Count	Bars
Soft spring on to L.F. raising R.F. to 5th position (aerial) rear and turning to right.	1	
Hop on L.F.	2	
Soft spring on R.F. raising L.F. to 5th position (aerial) rear, still turning to right.	3	
Hop on R.F. completing turn to right.	4	5
Repeat 5th bar three times more		6 and 8

5th to 8th bars may be done with common Schottische step.

HURNDILLA

Arranged by W. F. Hurndall.
Music Published by Francis, Day & Hunter Ltd.

Time : 3/4.   Tempo : 56 bars a minute.

Hold : No. 2 as described on page 7.

	Count	Bars
L.F. forward on ball of foot.	1	
R.F. to 4th position (aerial) in front.	2	
Hop on L.F.	3	1
Repeat 1st bar starting with R.F.		2
Step forward L.F.		3
Point R.F. to 4th position front.		4
R.F. back and close L.F. to 3rd position front.		5

	Count	Bars
R.F. back and close L.F. to 3rd position front without transferring weight.		6
Release lady's left hand, and solo Waltz outward, finishing to face wall and partner.		7 and 8
Holding partner's hands, balance to left on L.F.		9
Balance to right on R.F.		10
Releasing hands, balance back on L.F.		11
Balance forward R.F.		12
Adopt Waltz hold.		
Waltz Natural Turns.		13-16

IMPERIAL WALTZ

Arranged by J. Powell.

Music published by Francis, Day & Hunter Ltd.

Time : 3/4.   Tempo : 48 bars a minute.

Hold : No. 2 as described on page 7.

	Bars
Solo Waltz outward (reverse), starting with L.F.	1 and 2
Rejoin hands, L.F. forward. Point R.F. in 4th position front.	3 and 4
Solo Waltz inward (natural), starting with R.F.	5 and 6
Rejoin hands, R.F. forward. Point L.F. in 4th position front.	7 and 8
Pas de Valse, starting with L.F.	9
Balance forward on R.F.	10
Glide L.F. back against Line of Dance. Place right toe behind left heel and *Pivot* on balls of both feet to face partner, finishing with R.F. in 3rd position front.	11
Glide R.F. to side against L.O.D. and point L.F. to 5th position front.	12
Adopt Waltz hold.	
Waltz Natural Turns.	13-16

JAZZ TWINKLE

Arranged by J. Finnigan.

Music published by B. Feldman & Co. Ltd.

Time : 4/4.   Tempo : 32 bars a minute.

Hold : No. 3 as described on page 7.

	Count	Bars
Two steps forward, L.F., R.F., swaying first right and then left.	S.S	1
Twinkle as follows :		
L.F. back.	Q	
Close R.F. to L.F.	Q	
L.F. forward.	S	2
Repeat 1st and 2nd bars, starting with R.F. to finish facing diagonally to wall.	S.S.Q.Q.S	3 and 4
Chassé sideways, diagonally to centre : L.F., R.F., L.F.	Q.Q.S	5
Cross R.F. over L.F.	S	
L.F. to side, turning at end of step to face diagonally to wall against L.O.D.	S	6
Repeat 5th and 6th bars diagonally to wall against L.O.D. with R.F.	Q.Q.S.S.S	7 and 8
During the following scissors movement the gentleman is immediately behind the lady :—		
Cross L.F. over R.F., with slight dip, still moving diagonally to wall against L.O.D.	S	
Point R.F. to side, turning to face diagonally to centre.	S	9
Cross R.F. over L.F. with slight dip.	S	
Point L.F. to side, turning to face diagonally to wall against L.O.D.	S	10
Repeat last two bars, finishing to face L.O.D.	S.S.S.S	11 and 12
Partners now in starting position :—		
L.F. forward.	S	

	Count	Bars
R.F. forward, at the same time raising L.F. behind and looking over left shoulder.	S	13
Balance back on to L.F.	S	
R.F. back, raising L.F. in front and looking down at the toe.	S	14
Chassé to left. L.F., R.F., L.F.	Q.Q.S	15
Chassé to right : R.F., L.F., R.F.	Q.Q.S	16

KING'S WALTZ

Arranged by A. E. Brown.

Music published by Francis, Day & Hunter Ltd.

Time : 3/4.   Tempo : 48 bars a minute.

Hold : No. 2 as described on page 7.

	Count	Bars
Pas de Valse forward, starting with L.F.	1, 2, 3	1
Pas de Valse forward, starting with R.F.	1, 2, 3	2
(Lady half Reverse Turn starting with L.F.) Partners now side by side, gentleman facing L.O.D. lady backing L.O.D., gentleman's right hand holding lady's left hand and gentleman's left hand holding lady's right hand.		
L.F. forward.	1, 2, 3	3
R.F. forward with slight dip. (Lady : L.F. back preparing to turn to face partner.)	1, 2, 3	4
Two *Pas de Valse* forward, turning lady under right arm.	1, 2, 3 1, 2, 3	5 and 6

(Lady dances one Natural Waltz Turn, turning under gentleman's arm.)

Finish facing each other, gentleman back to centre, lady facing centre, both hands joined with arms fully extended.

41

	Count	Bars
L.F. to side, close R.F. to L.F. in 3rd position front.	1, 2, 3	7
Repeat 7th bar.		8
Adopt Waltz hold.		
Half Natural Waltz Turn and *Pas de Valse*, finishing to face L.O.D.		9 and 10
One *Pas de Valse* forward and half Natural Waltz Turn.		11 and 12
Four bars Natural Waltz Turn, opening out during last bar, ready to restart the sequence.		13-16

THE LADBROKE

Arranged by G. Chester.

Music published by Reid Bros. Ltd.

Time : 4/4.   Tempo : 28 bars a minute.

Hold : No. 3 as described on page 7.

	Count	Bars
L.F. forward.	S	
R.F. forward.	S	1
Spanish Corté as follows :		
L.F. forward, turning body to left to face diagonally to centre.	Q	
R.F. a small step to side.	Q	
Close L.F. to R.F., turning body to face L.O.D.	Q	
R.F. back.	Q	2
The head should be facing L.O.D. throughout, the body making an eighth turn to the left and back with a slight swagger.		
L.F. forward.	S	
Point R.F. in 4th position front.	S	3
R.F. forward, *pivoting* half turn to right to face against L.O.D.	S	
Point L.F. 4th position front against L.O.D.	S	4

	Count	Bars
Repeat first four bars, gentleman releasing lady's hands for *Pivot* turn to right in last bar.	`	5-8
Resuming original hold *Chassé* forward : L.F., R.F., L.F. with slight dip on 3rd step.	Q.Q.S	9
Chassé forward : R.F., L.F., R.F. with slight dip on 3rd step.	Q.Q.S	10
L.F. forward.	S	
Point R.F. in 4th position front.	S	11
R.F. forward.	S	
Point L.F. in 4th position front.	S	12
L.F. across in front of R.F.	S	
Point R.F. in rear intermediate	S	13
R.F. across in front of L.F.	S	
Point L.F. in rear intermediate.	S	14
Point L.F. forward turning lady under right arm. (Lady crosses L.F. well over R.F. and *Pivots*, making a complete turn to right under gentleman's right arm, finishing with weight on R.F.)	S.S	15
Repeat Spanish Corté as in 2nd bar.		16

MARINE FOUR STEP

Arranged by James Finnigan.

Music published by Francis, Day & Hunter Ltd.

Time : 2/4 or 6/8.   Tempo : 54-56 bars a minute.

Hold : No. 2 as described on page 7.

	Bars
L.F. forward, R.F. forward, L.F. forward (running steps). Hop on L.F., raising R.F. to fourth position (aerial).	1 and 2
Repeat first two bars backward, starting with R.F.	3 and 4

Pas de Basque outward and inward.   5 and 6

Release hands.

Solo Waltz : Gentleman to the left, Lady to the right and finish facing each other, joining hands with arms extended.   7 and 8

Three steps forward in *Promenade Position* along the L.O.D., pivoting on last step to face against L.O.D.   9 and 10

Repeat 9th and 10th bars against L.O.D. starting with R.F. pivoting on last step to face L.O.D.   11 and 12

Adopt Waltz Hold—Natural Waltz Turn.   13-16

THE MAXINA

Arranged by Madame Low-Hurndall.

Music published by Francis, Day & Hunter Ltd.

Time : 4/4.   Tempo : 32 bars a minute.

Hold : No. 3 as described on page 7.

Both lady and gentleman start on the same foot.

	Count	Bars
Glide L.F. diagonally forward, swaying to left and brush R.F. to L.F.	S	
Glide R.F. diagonally forward, swaying to right and brush L.F. to R.F.	S	1
Repeat 1st bar.		2
Chassé diagonally forward, starting with L.F. and swaying to left	Q.Q.S	3
Repeat 3rd bar, starting with R.F. and swaying to right.		4
Two steps forward (on balls of feet) : L.F., R.F.	S.S	5
Pivot on R.F. to face against L.O.D. and step through with L.F.	S	
Point R.F. to 4th position front against L.O.D.	S	6

	Count	Bars

Repeat 5th and 6th bars, starting with R.F. and *pivoting* to left, finishing with L.F. pointing along L.O.D.

7 and 8

Very small step forward on heel of L.F. with toe raised, starting to turn to left.

Q

Close R.F. to 3rd position rear still turning. (Body inclines towards front foot with left arm lowered and right arm raised.)

Q

Repeat above movement.

9

Repeat 9th bar three times, completing one full turn, arms back in starting position.

10-12

Two steps forward (on balls of feet) : L.F., R.F., turning to right and relaxing right knee on 2nd step.

S.S   13

Short step forward on heel of L.F. with toe raised. Close R.F. to L.F. in 3rd position rear. Point left toe in front of right heel.

Q.Q.S   14

Repeat 13th and 14th bars.

15 and 16

Two steps forward : L.F., R.F.

S.S   17

L.F. to side, turning to face wall, and turning lady under left arm.

S

Close R.F. to L.F.

S   18

Adopt Waltz hold.

Two Rotary *Chassés* (to right) starting with L.F., and making a complete turn.

Q.Q.S.Q.Q.S   19 and 20

Repeat 19th and 20th bars twice, finishing in original position.

21-24

ON LEAVE FOXTROT

Arranged by Mary Cheshire.

Time : 4/4.   Tempo : 32 bars a minute.

Hold : No. 1 as described on page 7.

	Count	Bars
Two steps forward L.F., R.F., with heel lead.	S.S	1
Chassé forward : L.F., R.F., L.F.	Q.Q.S	2
Repeat 1st and 2nd bars, starting with R.F.		3 and 4
Two steps forward : L.F., R.F.	S.S	5
Twinkle : Transfer weight to L.F. and close R.F. to L.F., L.F. forward.	Q.Q.S	6
Repeat 5th and 6th bars, starting on R.F., turning to right on last step into *Promenade Position* facing L.O.D.		7 and 8
Two steps forward along L.O.D. in *Promenade Position*, L.F., R.F., *Pivoting* to right on last step.	S.S	9
Cross L.F. over R.F. and run three steps against L.O.D. : L.F., R.F., L.F.	Q.Q.S	10
Bending left knee slightly, extend R.F. against L.O.D., at same time turning to face L.O.D.	S	
Raise R.F. to 4th position (aerial) forward.	S	11
Run three steps forward : R.F., L.F., R.F. in *Promenade Position*.	Q.Q.S	12
Release hold and step back towards centre : L.F., R.F.	S.S	13
(Lady steps forward towards wall : L.F., R.F.)		
Two steps forward towards partner : L.F., R.F.	S.S	14
Adopt original hold.		
Slow rotary (Natural) turn : L.F., R.F., L.F., R.F., finishing to face L.O.D.	S.S.S.S	15 and 16

ORIENTAL MAZURKA

Arranged by Tom Almond.

Music published by W. Paxton & Co.

Time : 3/4.   Tempo : 42 bars a minute.

Hold : No. 2 as described on page 7.

	Bars
Pas de Valse forward : L.F., R.F., L.F.	1
Glide R.F. forward. Close L.F. to R.F. in 3rd position rear. Hop lightly on L.F. and *fouette* with R.F., bringing it back to *aerial position* over L. instep.	2
Half Waltz turn inwards, starting with R.F. Join both hands and face against L.O.D., rear hands above the head and front hands low.	3
Glide L.F. back. Close R.F. to L.F. in 3rd position front. Look over lowered arms towards closing foot.	4
Repeat bars 1-4, starting with R.F. against L.O.D.	5-8
Adopt Waltz hold.	
Repeat 2nd bar, starting with L.F.	9
Natural Waltz turn.	10 and 11
Repeat 4th bar.	12
Natural Waltz Turn.	13-16

PRIDE OF ERIN WALTZ

Arranged by Charles Wood.

Time : 3/4.   Tempo : 48 bars a minute.

Starting position : Gentleman facing wall.

Hold : No. 5 as described on page 8.

	Bars
L.F. to side along L.O.D. in *Promenade Position.*	1
Cross R.F. over L.F.	2
Chassé to left : L.F., R.F., L.F., pivoting inward on last step and pointing R.F. against L.O.D.	3 and 4
Repeat bars 1-4 in the opposite direction, finishing the point along L.O.D.	5-8
(When pointing R.F. left hand is raised above the shoulder. When pointing L.F., right hand is raised above the shoulder.)	
Turning inward cross L.F. over R.F. against L.O.D.	9

Point R.F. against L.O.D. 10

(On 9th and 10th bars raise left hand and lower right hand.)

Cross R.F. over L.F. 11

Point L.F. along L.O.D., raising right hand and lowering left hand. 12

Gentleman releases lady's right hand and retains her left hand in his right hand. Waltz half Reverse Turn outward to left. 13

(Lady makes half Natural Turn outwards.)

Now back to back, both hands joined. Side R.F. and close L.F. to R.F. in 3rd position front without transfering weight. 14

Gentleman releases lady's left hand and retains her right hand in his left hand. Waltz half a turn outwards to the left. (Lady turns to right.) 15

Partners now face each other with both hands joined.

R.F. to side against L.O.D., close L.F. to R.F. in 3rd position front. 16

Balancé forward on L.F. towards wall on left side of lady. 17

Balancé back on R.F. towards centre. Gentleman retains lady's right hand in his left hand. 18

Half Reverse Waltz Turn to opposite places, turning lady under left arm. (Lady starts with R.F. and makes half Natural Turn.) 19

R.F. back a small step. Close L.F. without transferring weight. 20

Repeat bars 17-20 back to places. 21-24

(During the *Allemande,* gentleman holds his right hand on hip and lady's left hand holds skirt.)

Parallel Chassé to left starting with L.F. along L.O.D. 25

Swing R.F. over L.F. 26

Repeat 25th and 26th bars, starting with R.F., against L.O.D. 27 and 28

Adopt Waltz hold.

Waltz two Natural Turns. 29-32

LA RINKA

Arranged by W. F. Hurndall.

Music published by W. Paxton & Co. Ltd.

Time : 3/4.   Tempo : 48 bars a minute.

Hold : No. 6 as described on page 8.

	Bars
Both glide R.F. diagonally forward to right and close L.F. to 3rd position rear.	1
Repeat 1st bar without transferring weight on 2nd step.	2
Repeat 1st and 2nd bars diagonally forward to left, starting with L.F.	3 and 4
Glide R.F. diagonally forward to right and brush L.F. to R.F.	5
Repeat 5th bar, starting with L.F.	6
Repeat 6th bar, starting with R.F.	7
Repeat 7th bar, starting with L.F. with quarter *Pivot* inward to face partner, and close R.F. to 3rd position front without transferring weight, at same time bowing to partner and releasing left hands.	8
(Lady : L.F. back and curtsey.)	
Waltz half Natural Turn, R.F., L.F., R.F., to opposite places, and balance back on L.F.	9 and 10
(Lady : Half Reverse Turn, L.F., R.F., L.F., turning under the gentleman's right arm and balance back R.F.)	
Repeat 9th and 10th bars back to places.	11 and 12
Join opposite hands.	
Glide R.F. to side against L.O.D. and close L.F. to 3rd position front, then repeat these two steps, without change of weight.	13 and 14
Repeat 13th and 14th bars, starting with L.F. along L.O.D. but changing weight on last step.	15 and 16
Adopt Waltz hold.	
Natural Waltz, finishing in original position.	17-24

Note : A skating action should be used on all steps in bars 1-8.

LA ROSA

Arranged by George Chester.

Music published by Reid Bros.

Time : 3/4.   Tempo : 48 bars a minute.

Hold : No. 5 as described on page 8.

	Bars
Three steps along L.O.D. in *Promenade Position* : L.F., R.F., L.F.	1-3
Turn inward to face against L.O.D., pointing R.F.	4
Solo Waltz outward against L.O.D., starting with R.F., gentleman turning to right and lady to left.	5 and 6
Adopt Waltz hold.	
R.F. forward against L.O.D.	7
Point L.F. back and hold position, facing against L.O.D., with left arm raised.	8
Join both hands, turning to face L.O.D. (lady back to L.O.D.), L.F. forward. R.F. forward outside partner with slight relaxation.	9 and 10
Turning on R.F. to face against L.O.D., L.F. back, R.F. back with slight relaxation.	11 and 12
(Lady steps forward with L.F. on gentleman's left side.)	
Adopt Waltz hold.	
Waltz four bars of Natural Turn.	13-16

SERENATA

Arranged by Albert Cowan.

Time : 2/4.   Tempo : 38 bars a minute.

Starting position : Gentleman facing Line of Dance.

Hold : No. 1 as described on page 7.

	Count	Bars
L.F. forward along L.O.D. Point R.F. forward.	S.S	1
R.F. forward along L.O.D. Point L.F. forward.	S.S.	2
Repeat 1st and 2nd bars, turning into *Promenade Position* on last step to face L.O.D.		3 and 4
Two steps forward L.F., R.F. in *Promenade Position*, starting to turn to right on last step.	S.S	5
L.F. to side across L.O.D. still turning.	Q	
Close R.F. to L.F. (square to partner).	Q	6
L.F. back along L.O.D. turning to right.	S	
Still turning, small step to side with R.F. (Heels slightly apart.)	S	7
L.F. forward facing centre.	S	
Twinkle backward. (Start by transferring weight back over R.F.)	Q.Q.S	8
L.F. to left (a very small step). Close R.F. to L.F., turning to left	Q.Q	9 and 10
Repeat last two steps three more times to face L.O.D.	Q.Q.Q.Q.Q.Q	
Two steps forward : L.F., R.F.	S.S	11
Twinkle. (Start by transferring weight back over L.F.)	Q.Q.S	12
Repeat 11th and 12th bars, starting on R.F. and turning to right on last step.	S.S.Q.Q.S	13 and 14
Rotary chassé : L.F., R.F., L.F., R.F., L.F., R.F.	Q.Q.S.Q.Q.S	15 and 16

SQUARE TANGO

Time : 2/4.   Tempo : 32 bars a minute.

Hold : No. 4 as described on page 8.

	Count	Bars
L.F. forward.	S	
R.F. to side.	Q	
Close L.F. to R.F.	Q	1
R.F. back.	S	
L.F. to side.	Q	
Close R.F. to L.F.	Q	2
L.F. to side, a long step.	S	
Close R.F. to L.F. without transferring weight.	S	3
R.F. to side, a long step.	S	
Close L.F. to R.F. without transferring weight.	S	4
Repeat above four bars.		5-8
Two steps forward : L.F., R.F.	S.S	
Two steps forward : L.F., R.F.	Q.Q	
Repeat above two movements.	S.S.Q.Q	9-11
L.F. forward.	S	
R.F. forward, turning to face wall.	S	12
L.F. to side and slightly back.	S	
R.F. back to centre.	S	13
L.F. forward towards wall.	S	
Four rotary walks starting with R.F. making three-quarters of a turn to face L.O.D.	S.S.S.S	
Balance back on R.F.	S	14-16

TANGO WALTZ

Arranged by C. J. Daniels.

Time : 3/4.   Tempo : 48 bars a minute.

Hold : No. 1 as described on page 7.

	Bars
Four steps back towards centre : L.F., R.F., L.F., R.F., swaying to left and right alternately.	1-4

	Bars
Repeat bars 1-4 forward towards wall.	5-8
L.F. to side along L.O.D. Close R.F. to 3rd position front.	9
L.F. to side along L.O.D. Close R.F. to 3rd position front without transferring weight.	10
Repeat 9th and 10th bars to right against L.O.D.	11 and 12
Three bars Natural Waltz Turn and one bar *Pas de Valse*, finishing with R.F. in 3rd position rear, facing L.O.D. in *Promenade Position*. (Lady dances four bars Natural Waltz Turn, finishing with R.F. in 3rd position front.)	13-16
L.F. forward in *Promenade Position* along L.O.D.	17
R.F. forward and across in *Promenade Position* with slight relaxation of the left knee.	18
L.F. forward. Close R.F. to L.F. in 5th position rear without transferring weight.	19
R.F. back. Close L.F. to 5th position front without transferring weight.	20
Repeat bars 17-20.	21-24
Repeat bars 9-12.	25-28
Natural Waltz Turn.	29-32

VALSE SUPERBE

Arranged by Charles W. Gardner.

Music published by Francis, Day & Hunter Ltd.

Time : 3/4.   Tempo : 46 bars a minute.

Hold : No. 2 as described on page 7.

	Bars
Half Reverse Turn starting with L.F. Partners finish back to back and join both hands.	1
R.F. to side along L.O.D. Close L.F. to R.F.	2
R.F. to side along L.O.D. Close L.F. to R.F. without transferring weight.	3
Half Reverse Turn against L.O.D. starting with L.F., gentleman releasing lady's left hand but retaining her right hand. Partners now face each other and join both hands.	4

53

	Bars
R.F. to side against L.O.D. Close L.F. to R.F.	5
R.F. to side against L.O.D. Close L.F. to R.F. without transferring weight.	6
Solo Reverse Turn, starting with L.F.	7 and 8

(Lady solo Natural Turn, starting with R.F.)
Partners now in starting position.

Two *Pas de Valse* forward along L.O.D. starting
with L.F. and finishing to face partner with R.F.
in 3rd position front, facing wall with both hands
joined. 9 and 10

L.F. to side along L.O.D.   Close R.F. to L.F.
without transferring weight. 11

R.F. to side against L.O.D.   Close L.F. to R.F.
without transferring weight. 12

Adopt Waltz hold.

Natural Waltz Turns 13-16

VIENNESE SEQUENCE WALTZ

Arranged by Jack Mercer.

Time : 3/4.   Tempo : 54 bars a minute.

Hold : No. 7 as described on page 8.

Both start with the L.F. Lady and gentleman use the same feet
for the first eight bars. For the remainder, lady contra.

	Bars
L.F. a short step to side. Swing R.F. across L.F.	1
R.F. a short step to side. Swing L.F. across R.F.	2
Pas de Valse forward, starting with L.F.	3
Pas de Valse forward, starting with R.F.	4

Repeat above 4 bars, gentleman turning to face
wall at end of 8th bar (lady on 8th bar makes ¾ turn
to right on R.F. to face centre, count 1, 2, closes
L.F. to R.F. count 3). 5-8

Adopt Waltz Hold, but with lady slightly to left
of gentleman. From now on lady's feet are contra.

L.F. forward outside lady's left side and lock R.F.
behind L.F. without transferring weight. 9

R.F. back (lady L.F. forward outside gentleman's left side) and lock L.F. in front of R.F. without transferring weight.

L.F. forward outside lady's left side, completing first half of Reverse Turn, preparing to step outside lady's right side towards centre.

R.F. forward outside lady's right side and swivel half turn to right to face wall.

Repeat bars 9-12 to finish facing L.O.D. side by side.

Solo Waltz outward making ¾ turn (gentleman reverse, lady natural). Gentleman finishes facing wall holding both lady's hands.

Pas de basque to left.

Pas de basque to right.

Solo Waltz outward, gentleman reverse, lady natural.

Taking both partner's hands, balance forward on L.F. locking R.F. behind L.F. without transferring weight. (Lady balances forward on R.F.) Left shoulder to left shoulder.

R.F. back, closing L.F. to R.F. without transferring weight.

Adopt Waltz hold.

Complete four bars of Natural Waltz Turn.

Gentleman remains stationary, leading his partner across to his left side and back again, on last beat opening out to starting position. (Lady dances two *Pas de Valse*, starting with her R.F. across partner to partner's left side, turning inwards to her left on the 5th and 6th steps. Repeat two *Pas de Valse* back to partner's right side, opening out to starting position on the last step. A loose Waltz hold should be maintained throughout this movement.)

	Bars
	10
	11
	12
	13-16
	17 and 18
	19
	20
	21 and 22
	23
	24
	25-28
	29-32

YEARNING SAUNTER

Arranged by H. Boyle, Senior.

Time : 4/4.   Tempo : 26 bars a minute.

Hold : No. 4 as described on page 8.

	Bars
Four steps forward along L.O.D., starting with L.F.	1 and 2
Balance back on L.F. Balance forward on R.F. and repeat.	3 and 4
Repeat bars 1-4.	5-8
L.F. over R.F. ⎫ Scissors movement. R.F. over L.F. ⎭	9 and 10
Repeat 9th and 10th bars.	11 and 12
Chassé, starting with L.F.	13
Chassé, starting with R.F.	14
Rotary *Chassé* turn : L.F., R.F., L.F., R.F., L.F. R.F.	15 and 16

SQUARE DANCES

In all Square Dances, except where otherwise stated, close in *first position*. When working solo or in lines start with the right foot. When in pairs start with the outside foot.

THE CALEDONIANS

	Bars
Eight bar introduction.	8
	—

Figure One

	Bars
First and second couples give right hands across and starting with L.F. pass half round clockwise (*Moulinet*).	4
Then give left hands across and pass half round anti-clockwise (*Moulinet*) and return to places.	4
Set to partners and turn.	8
Ladies' Chain.	8
First and second couples *promenade* to opposite places.	4
Return to places with *half right and left*.	4
	—
	32
This is repeated by the third and fourth couples.	32
	—
	64
	—

Figure Two

Introduction. 8

___

First gentleman advances and retires alone twice. 8

All gentlemen set to corner ladies and turn, with propelled pivot. 8

All couples *promenade* the set anti-clockwise, the gentleman taking his new partner back to his own place. 8

___

24

Second, third and fourth gentlemen repeat the figure until the ladies have regained their original partners and places. 72

___

96

___

Figure Three

Introduction. 8

___

First lady and second gentleman advance to centre. Retire one step with *balancé,* step forward with *balancé,* and turn with propelled pivot and retire to places. 8

First couple lead through to centre to opposite places. Second couple passing them on the outside. In returning to place, the second couple lead through the centre, while the first couple pass on the outside (*le Tiroir*). 8

All set to corners, turn with propelled pivot and retire to places. 8

All couples join hands to form Grand Circle, advance, retire and turn partners. 8

___

32

This figure is repeated by the second, third and fourth lady and the opposite gentleman, leading in turn. 96

___

128

___

Figure Four

Introduction.   8

First lady and second gentleman advance to the centre, turning inwards on count 3 to face centre. Close on count 4 in 3rd position rear.   2

Second lady and first gentleman advance to the centre.   2

Partners turn with propelled pivot, finishing in places.   4

The four ladies move one place to the right with seven walking steps and a close.   4

The four gentlemen move one place to the left (passing in front) with seven walking steps and a close.   4

The ladies repeat this movement to the right.   4

The gentlemen repeat this movement to the left.   4

Partners are now in opposite places.

All couples *promenade* to places and turn with propelled pivot.   8

                                                                32

The whole is repeated by second lady and first gentleman, third lady and fourth gentleman, fourth lady and third gentleman.   96

                                                               128

Figure Five

Introduction.   8

First couple *promenade* round inside the set.   8

The four ladies advance to the centre, curtsey and retire.   .   4

The four gentlemen advance, turn to face partners and bow.   4

All set to partners and turn with propelled pivot.   8

Grand Chain half round, couples finishing in opposite places.   Balance forward and back.   8

Couples *promenade* to places and turn with propelled pivot.

All cast off, i.e., partners join left hands and gentlemen pass their ladies to the gentleman who was on their left.   Gentlemen then present right hands to lady who was on their right.   Return to own places by again presenting left hand to partner (Corner Chain).

8

—

48

Repeat the whole, second, third and fourth couples leading in turn.

144

—

192

All promenade to places and turn with *propelled pivot.*

8

—

200

—

THE CARNIVAL

Arranged by H. R. Johnson.

Music published by Francis, Day & Hunter, Ltd.

Time : 4/4.   Tempo : 28 bars a minute.

Carnival is a square dance for four couples.   All form sets as in Lancers.

Figure One: *Barn Dance Movement*

Bars

The Barn Dance movement is used throughout this figure, i.e.,

L.F. forward.   Close R.F. to L.F. in 3rd position rear.

L.F. forward.   Hop on L.F. bringing R.F. to 4th position front (aerial).

Repeat, starting with R.F.

Introduction. Bow and curtsey to partners then to corners.

60

Couples 1 and 2 turn to right face corner couple.
Couples 3 and 4 turn to left face corner couple.
All couples advance and retire to corner couple,
with Barn Dance Movement. 2
All couples cross to opposite places with half
right and left. 2
All couples advance and retire. 2
Turn partners with propelled pivot. 2
Ladies' chain. 8

On regaining his partner, the gentleman, who is
holding his partner's left hand in his left hand,
changes it into his right hand and faces the next
position, i.e., 1st couple is now in 3rd couple's place,
and faces towards 2nd couple's place, which is
occupied by the 4th couple.

The movement is repeated three times.

1st and 2nd couples move to each place round the
set in anti-clockwise direction.

3rd and 4th couples will move round in clockwise
direction.

Figure Two: *Marching Movement*

Time : 2/4. Tempo : 56 bars a minute.

All join hands in a circle, gallopade the set
round to places in clockwise direction. 1-8
All advance to centre raising hands, and retire. 9-12
Gentlemen turn partners to the centre to face
them ; all ladies back to back in the centre. 13 and 14
Bow and curtsey to partner ; all join hands in
two circles. 15 and 16
Both circles gallopade to the right, gentlemen
anti-clockwise and ladies clockwise. 17-22
Gentleman takes partner's right hand and turns
her under his arm, thus changing places with her.
Gentlemen now back to back in the centre, ladies
facing partners form outside circle, join hands in
two circles. 23 and 24
All gallopade to left, gentlemen anti-clockwise,
ladies clockwise. 25-30

Bow and curtsey to partners, gentleman stepping to left, ladies to right, as in Latchford Schottische. 31 and 32
Waltz round the set. 33-48

Figure Three: *The Polka Movement*
Time : 2/4. Tempo : 48.

Use Polka step throughout, i.e. : Hop on R.F. Step on L.F., close R.F. to L.F. Spring on to L.F. Repeat on opposite foot.

Turn to face partners, join right hands.

Grand chain as in Lancers, slight acknowledgment to partner on meeting in opposite places, grand chain back to places, at end of which gentlemen take partners' left hand in their right hands and give left hands across to opposite gentlemen forming a *moulin* (grand cross) getting into position with two polka steps. 1-16

All polka forward anti-clockwise (very small steps), to reach opposite places. Then bow and curtsey to partners. 17-24

Take partner in Waltz hold and polka half round the set to places. 25-30

1st and 2nd couples polka on to face 3rd and 4th couples as in visiting figure in Lancers. 31-32

Give right hands across (*moulinet*).

Take four polka steps forward. 33-36

Turn about, give left hands across, take three polka steps forward. 37-39

1st and 2nd couples fall back to places joining hands in large circle. 40

Polka in circle round the set clockwise to places. 41-48

The above 48 bars are repeated, on bars 31 and 32, 3rd couple visits 2nd couple, 4th couple visits 1st couple. Bar 40 : 3rd and 4th couples fall back to places. 49-96

All couples, with inside hands joined, Berlin Polka* to centre of set. 97 and 98

	Bars
All couples Berlin Polka back to places.	99 and 100
Taking Waltz hold rotary polka round the set to opposite places.	101-104
Repeat Berlin Polka to centre and back.	105 and 106
Resume Waltz hold and rotary polka to places.	107-110

Gentleman holding lady's left hand in his right hand. Polka step to centre starting with hop on R.F.   1

Hop on L.F. pointing R.F. to centre. Hop again on L.F. turning to right to face out of the set pointing R.F. forward.   2

Changing hands repeat in opposite direction starting with hop on L.F.   3 and 4

* Berlin Polka. Gentleman's steps. Lady contra.

Figure Four: *Waltz Movement*

Time : 3/4.   Tempo : 48.

All face corners joining right hands. All balance forward and backward starting R.F.   1 and 2

Gentlemen turn ladies with *allemande* under right arm to finish back to back in centre of set.   3 and 4

Repeat above four bars, gentlemen changing places with ladies.   5-8

Adopt Waltz hold.

Waltz the set.   9-22

Bow and curtsey to partners.   23 and 24

Repeat above 24 bars three times, gentleman having a new partner each time. He dances with his own partner the 4th time.

The music finishes with 4 bar finale, gentlemen turn partners *allemande* to centre, bow and curtsey, offer right arm to partner and escort her to her seat.

THE LANCERS

Figure One: *La Rose*

Eight bar introduction :
    Gentlemen bow and ladies curtsey to partners.   4
    Gentlemen bow and ladies curtsey to corners.   4

    —
    8
    —

First lady and second gentleman advance to centre, starting with R.F., step backwards with L.F. closing R.F. to 3rd position front, step forward R.F. closing L.F. to 3rd position rear. Turn with *propelled pivot* and retire to places.   8

First couple lead through the centre to the opposite places. 2nd couple passing them on the outside. In returning to places second couple lead through to centre while first couple pass on the outside (*le Tiroir*).   8

All set to corners, turn with *propelled pivot* and retire to places.   8

    —
    24

This figure is repeated three times. Second, third and fourth lady and the opposite gentlemen leading in turn.   72

    —
    96
    —

Figure Two: *La Ladoiska*

Eight bar introduction.   8

    —

First and second couples advance and retire. Gentlemen advance leading lady round to face him. (Ladies now back to back in the centre.) Bow and curtsey.   8

Both couples set and turn with partners with propelled pivot.   8

Third and fourth couples separate and join hands with the first and second couples forming top and bottom lines.   All advance and retire and turn partners in places.   8

—

24

This figure is repeated with third and fourth couples.   24

—

48

=

48

Repeat above 48 bars.   48

—

96

—

Figure Three: *La Dorset*

Eight bar introduction.   8

—

The four ladies advance, curtsey and retire.   The four gentlemen advance and join hands in a ring, the ladies linking the gentlemen's arms.   8

—

All move to the left, using *Propelled Pivot*, finishing in own places.   8

The four gentlemen advance to the centre, retire, re-advance, bow to their ladies and give their left hands across to each other.   8

Gentlemen place their right arms round their ladies' waists, promenade forward and retire to places.   8

—

32

Repeat above 32 bars.   32

—

64

—

Figure Four: *L'Etoile*

Eight bar introduction. 8

First and second couples advance to visit couple on their right, acknowledge, and move on to visit the couple on their left. 8

First and fourth couples and second and third give right hands across and move round seven steps, then give left hands across and move round seven steps (*Moulinet*) and close, transferring weight. 8

· Form two circles of four. *Propelled pivot* round and retire to places. 8

——

24

These 24 bars are repeated by the same couples visiting first to the left and moving on to the right. 24

——

48

The whole 48 bars are repeated by the third and fourth couples. 48

——

96

——

Figure Five: *Les Lanciers*

No introduction, chord only.

Grand chain : Couples face each other and join right hands, move round giving left and right hands alternately. On meeting partner in opposite places, balance forwards and rearwards, continue chain round to own places. 16

First couple leading round inside the set and finishing in their own place facing outwards. Third couple falls in behind and then fourth couple, second couple remaining in place, forming two lines. 8

The ladies and gentlemen move sideways, across to each other's places, the ladies passing in front of the gentlemen. (*Chassé Croisé.*) *Balancé* forwards and backwards. Re-crossing, *balancé* forwards and backwards. 8

Ladies and gentlemen lead inwards and then counter march outwards falling back into two side lines. 8

The lines advance and retire, all advance to partners and turn with *propelled pivot* in own places.   8

    ───
    48
This is repeated three times.   144
Follow with Grand Chain. Finish with Propelled Pivot, with partner in place.   16

    ───
    208
    ───

The order of falling in is as follows :

(1) 1st	(2) 2nd	(3) 3rd	(4) 4th
3rd	4th.	2nd	1st
4th	3rd	1st	2nd
2nd	1st	4th	3rd

QUADRILLES
Figure One: *Le Pantalon*

Bars

Introduction :
    Gentlemen bow and ladies curtsey to their partners.   4
    Gentlemen bow and ladies curtsey to the corners.   4

    ───
    8
    ───

First and second couples *right and left*. Finish facing partner.   8
    Set to partners and turn.   8
    Ladies' chain.   8
    Both couples promenade to the opposite places.   4
    Return to places with a *half right and left*.   4

    ───
    32
    ───

The above is repeated by the third and fourth couples.   32

    ───
    64
    ───

Figure Two: *L'Eté*

Eight bar introduction.   8

    —

First and second couples advance and retire, cross
over to opposite places (*Traversé*).   8
Both couples advance and retire, re-cross to own
places. (*Retraversé.*)   8
Set to partners and turn.   8

    —

     24

These 24 bars are repeated by the third and fourth
couples.   24

    —

     48

Repeat entire 48 bars.   48

    —

     96

    —

Figure Three: *La Poule*

Eight bar introduction.   8

    —

First lady and second gentleman cross to opposite
places, touching right hands. Re-cross, joining left
hands and giving right hands to partners.   8
Retaining hands all four balance forward and
backward towards own partners twice, leading
round to opposite places.   8
First lady and second gentleman advance and
retire. Re-advance, bow and curtsey and retire.   8
First and second couples advance and retire.
Half right and left back to own places.   8

     32

These 32 bars are repeated by each lady and
opposite gentleman in turn.   96

    —

     128

    —

Figure Four: *La Pastourelle*

Eight bar introduction. — 8

First couple advance and retire. Re-advance, the gentleman leaving his partner with the opposite gentleman. (Both ladies facing centre.) — 8

Second gentleman advances and retires with both ladies (first gentleman retires as they advance). Re-advance, leaving both ladies with the first gentleman. — 8

First gentleman advances and retires with both ladies (second gentleman retires). — 4

Line of three re-advance. Second gentleman also advances, and all join hands, forming a circle in the centre of the set. — 4

All move half round with propelled pivot and retire to opposite places. Return to own places with a half right and left. — 8

—

32

These 32 bars are repeated three times, each couple leading in turn. — 96

—

128

—

.

Figure Five: *Flirtation*

Eight bar introduction. — 8

—

All join hands, forming a circle. Advance and retire and turn partners with *propelled pivot.* — 8

The four ladies advance to the centre, curtsey and retire. — 4

The four gentlemen advance to centre, bow, turning to left, bow to corner lady. — 4

All gentlemen set to corner, ladies turn with *propelled pivot.* — 8

All couples *promenade* the set, the gentleman taking his new partner back to his own place. — 8

—

32

These 32 bars are repeated three times, bringing
the ladies back to their original places. 96

The figure finishes with a grand circle, and turn
partners. 8

_____

136

_____

WALTZ COTILLION

Time : 3/4.   Tempo : 48 bars a minute.

Eight bar introduction :

Gentlemen bow and ladies curtsey to partners. 4

Gentlemen bow and ladies curtsey to corners. 4

___

8

===

First couple Waltz round inside the set, disengaging
at end of 15th bar. 16

First and second ladies Waltz anti-clockwise
across to opposite places, finishing with slight
salutation. 8

Third and fourth ladies repeat last 8 bars. 8

— 32

First and second gentlemen Waltz anti-clockwise
across to opposite places, finishing with slight
salutation. 8

Third and fourth gentlemen repeat last 8 bars. 8

First and second couples Waltz to places. 8

Third and fourth couples Waltz to places. 8

— 32

Waltz Chain.   All ladies and gentleman begin
with the right foot and execute a *Balancé* forward
and backward, and *Allemande,* the gentleman
making a Natural Waltz Turn while the lady makes
the rotory half of a Reverse Waltz Turn and a *Pas
de Valse.*   This movement is repeated with each

70

partner in turn (16 bars). The whole is then repeated, each couple starting from the opposite place in the set.

NOTE : The last *Allemande* is completed with the side couples divided from their partners in preparation for the next figure. 32

Top and Bottom Lines. Starting with the right foot, advance with *Pas de Valse* and *Balancé*, retire with *Pas de Valse* and *Pas Glissé*. 4

Advance with *Pas de Valse* : R.F., L.F., R.F. and L.F., R.F., L.F. Half Natural Waltz Turn and *Pas Glissé*. 4

Repeat last eight bars, finishing in own places. 8

All couples Waltz round the set. 16

— 32

128

The whole of the above is repeated three times, each couple leading in turn.

NOTE : When third or fourth couples lead, the lines are Side Lines. 384

512

Lightning Source UK Ltd.
Milton Keynes UK
20 August 2010
158729UK00001B/169/A